AF350651

Copyright Page

____

A Delicious Christmas: Beautiful Ways to Celebrate Christ
Copyright © 2024 by Kim Ruff Moore
All rights reserved. No part of this publication may be reproduced, stored in a retrieval system, or transmitted in any form or by any means—electronic, mechanical, photocopying, recording, or otherwise—without prior written permission from the publisher.

Scripture References
All Scripture quotations in this book are taken from the Holy Bible. Specific translations are noted alongside each verse where applicable. This list provides the references for all Scriptures used throughout *A Delicious Christmas*, celebrating the spirit of Christmas with reverence for God's Word.

- Psalm 34:8–"Otasteandseethatthe Lordisgood:blessedisthemanthattrustethin him."
- Hebrews 13:16–"Donotneglecttodogoodandtosharewhatyouhave,forsuch sacrifices are pleasing to God."
- Matthew 2:10–"Whentheysawthestar,theyrejoicedwithexceedinggreatjoy."
- Isaiah 9:6–"Foruntousachildisborn,untousasonisgiven:andthegovernment shall be upon his shoulder: and his name shall be called Wonderful, Counsellor, The mighty God, The everlasting Father, The Prince of Peace."

For additional information, please visit:
kimruffmoore.com
ruffmooremedia.com
Printed in the United States of America
979-8-3305-5944-2

This book is dedicated to all who cherish the beauty and joy of Christmas in their hearts and homes. May it inspire you to celebrate the season with a renewed appreciation for the love and grace of Christ.

Discover the Inspiring Works of Kim Ruff Moore
Kim Ruff Moore is a prolific author with over 90 titles in children's and adult literature. As the founder of the Please Read Project, she is dedicated to promoting literacy by donating her books to those in need.
Adult Books:

- Girl Mash the Gas: Stop Procrastinating
- Girl, Forgive Them and Move On
- I Still Have Joy (BestSeller)
- Never Put All Your Eggs in One Basket (Financial Wisdom)
- Waymaker
- Cuffed (MarriageReleasesGod'sFavor)

Serendipity
Secrets of a Successful Published Author
I Speak Life
Children's Books:

● Suzzie Mocha Series
● Pebo Pig Series
● Sergio the Mouse Series
● Otis the Brown Bear
● Spence Seven Series
● Land of Unicorns Series
● I Want to Sing Like Whitney
● Bria Gets New Braids
● Klohe's Favorite Things
● Oliver and the Ocean
● Love Brought Max Home
● A Horse Called Midnight
● Mommy, I Can Do It Series
● Faus the Fox Finds Fall Colors
● Elo the Elephant Forgets Everything
● And Many More!

Kim's books are available at Walmart, Barnes & Noble, Books-A-Million, and other major retailers. Explore her inspiring works at kimruffmoore.com and ruffmooremedia.com!

A Delicious Christmas: Beautiful Ways to Celebrate Christ

By Kim Ruff Moore

Table of Contents

Introduction: My Love for Christmas

I absolutely adore Christmas. Everything about it fills my heart with joy—the cozy pajamas, Christmas cards filled with love, twinkling lights, and especially the sweet aroma of holiday treats baking in the kitchen. The whole season feels like a celestial celebration, a time of good tidings, hope, and a reminder of the precious gift of Christ's birth. From heartwarming Hallmark movies to gatherings with loved ones, Christmas brings us moments to savor and share.

When my son Spencer was small, I used to go the extra mile to make the holidays so incredibly special. I loved seeing his eyes light up when he'd wake up to find our home transformed into a Christmas wonderland, complete with sparkling lights, festive garlands, and the warm aroma of treats baking in the kitchen. Spencer is 23 now, and those precious memories feel as vibrant today as they did back then.

There was such joy in creating traditions—decorating the tree together, baking cookies for Santa, and even our little ritual of reading the Christmas story on Christmas Eve. I'll always cherish those years. Watching his excitement and wonder during the holidays reminded me of how magical Christmas can be, especially when seen through the eyes of a child.

Of course, each stage of life is a blessing, and I'm blessed beyond measure to witness Spencer growing into an incredible young man. But there's something about Christmas that always brings those memories back, reminding me of the beauty of family and tradition.

To me, the holidays are truly delicious. There's divinity fudge, spiced cakes, and homemade candies, each bite a reminder of the season's sweetness. Christmas isn't just in the food and festivities, though—it's in the warmth of giving and the joyful remembrance of God's love for us. There's so much going on in the world, but Christmas invites us to pause, reflect, and embrace the good that still surrounds us. As the psalmist says, "O taste and see that the Lord is good" (Psalm 34:8), and I believe there's no better time to experience His goodness than this beautiful, festive season.

So, I invite you to join me in celebrating the birth of Christ as we savor each moment and every delicious blessing this season brings. Let's taste the sweetness of life, cherishing the joy and peace that Christmas offers.

Christmas has always held a special place in my heart. From the time I was a little child, something magical seemed to happen the moment December approached. The cold weather, the crispness of the air as winter sets in, brings about a sense of renewal, anticipation, and warmth, despite the dropping temperatures. I've always loved the way the world seems to glow with light and life in December—the streets adorned with twinkling lights, red and green decorations everywhere, and a sense of goodwill that radiates from the simplest of things. There's something about Christmas that brings out the best in people, even if only for a short time.

More than the gifts or the commercial side of it, I cherish the way families come together during the holiday season. It's a time of reunion and reflection, where we pause from our busy lives to be with one another, to laugh, eat, and remember what truly matters. The sight of children, wide-eyed with wonder, is one of the purest joys of Christmas. Their excitement at the prospect of Christmas morning is contagious, reminding us adults of the joy and innocence that the season brings.

The Beauty of Christmas Traditions

One of the things I look forward to the most each year is seeing entire neighborhoods transformed into festive wonderlands. As soon as the decorations go up, it feels like the world takes on a new form—a form that's more vibrant and alive. The bright red and green, traditional Christmas colors, are everywhere—on wreaths, trees, storefronts, and homes. Red, representing the sacrifice of Christ's love, and green, the eternal hope of salvation, blend together to create a visual symphony that stirs something deep within. For me, those colors are more than decoration; they symbolize the very heart of what Christmas means.

It's not just the decorations or the lights but the fact that almost every store closes on Christmas Day. I love that sense of reverence, that collective pause from the hustle and bustle. It's one of the few days in the year when it feels like the entire world stops—just for a moment—and remembers that there is something greater than all of us. The act of closing businesses, for me, symbolizes a time to reflect, a time for families to gather without distractions. It's as if the whole world acknowledges the sacredness of the day.

Christmas as a Time of Unity

Even in today's often divided world, Christmas has a way of uniting people from all walks of life. Whether or not everyone agrees on the exact details of the holiday or its origins, there's no denying the collective spirit that moves through communities during the season. Children eagerly await the break from school, anticipating not just the presents but the quality time with family and the joy of shared meals and traditions. It's a time when people seem to go out of their way to be kind to one another. You see it in the smiles of strangers as you pass them on the street, the extra effort that people put into helping others, and the general atmosphere of goodwill.

For me, Christmas embodies a deep sense of unity. Regardless of where you come from, what you believe, or what you celebrate, Christmas has become a day that transcends cultural and religious boundaries. The spirit of the holiday—the ideas of love, generosity, and togetherness—are universal. And for that, I love it all the more.

The Debate Over Celebrating Christmas

Yet, despite all the joy Christmas brings, there are those who feel conflicted about its celebration. Many people, even those who profess belief in Christ, refuse to celebrate Christmas for various reasons. I've heard some say they won't celebrate because Jesus never explicitly told us to commemorate His birth. Others point to the holiday's origins, arguing that Christmas has pagan roots and that its traditions are far removed from what Jesus represents. Some refuse to celebrate simply because they believe Christ wasn't born on December 25th.

To be honest, I've wrestled with these thoughts too. At first, it can be confusing to hear so many conflicting opinions about a holiday that brings so much joy. The arguments about pagan origins, the commercialism of modern-day Christmas, and even the uncertainty surrounding the exact birthdate of Jesus can all make one pause. But then, I remember the heart of the matter. What does it really mean to celebrate Christmas? Is it about the specific day? Is it about the traditions? Or is it about something much deeper?

What Christmas Means to Me
For me, the answer is simple: I celebrate Christmas because I believe in Jesus Christ. I may not know the exact day of His birth, but I know beyond a shadow of a doubt that He was born. He came into this world for a purpose, and that purpose was to save me and every person who has ever lived. The miracle of His birth is something worth celebrating. It's a reminder that God loved us so much that He sent His only Son into the world to save us from our sins. And that's something I want to rejoice in—every year, without fail.

Yes, it's true that Christmas, as we know it, has been shaped by centuries of traditions, some of which may have pagan origins. But for me, that doesn't take away from the heart of the holiday. Over time, Christmas has evolved into a day where people come together to celebrate something far bigger than themselves. It's a day of joy, love, and unity—a day where we reflect on the greatest gift ever given to humanity. I choose to see Christmas as a day set aside to remember and celebrate the birth of Christ. I choose to focus on the love He showed us, rather than the arguments over its exact date or origins.

Count Me In So yes, when it comes to Christmas, count me in. I'll be there celebrating with my family, sharing in the joy and peace that the season brings. I'll be the one decorating my home with red and green, lighting up the night with twinkling lights, and giving thanks for the greatest gift I've ever received—salvation through Christ. For me, Christmas is more than just a day on the calendar. It's a time to reflect on what matters most in life: faith, family, love, and hope. So, no matter what others may say or believe, I will continue to celebrate Christmas in my own way—knowing that the heart of the holiday is something eternal, something that transcends time, tradition, and debate.

I invite you and your family to join me in celebrating this season through cherished holiday festivities and time-honored traditions. Let's fill this December with warmth and wonder, from baking sweet treats together to sharing cozy nights with loved ones. There's something truly special about gathering in the kitchen, dusted in flour, as laughter mixes with the scents of cinnamon and cocoa.

So come along as we dive into the simple joys of the season. Whether it's baking cookies, singing carols, or cozying up by the fire, let's embrace every beautiful moment, savoring the sweetness of Christmas and celebrating the love and light it brings to our lives. May this holiday season fill your hearts and homes with peace, joy, and the deliciousness of life well-lived.

Pay It Forward

Christmas is often seen as a time for family gatherings, gift-giving, and celebration. But at its core, Christmas is about Jesus—the One who came to earth as a baby, destined to become the Savior of the world. His life was marked by love, compassion, and sacrifice, and His birth signifies the beginning of God's greatest gift to humanity. When we celebrate Christmas, we are celebrating the love of Jesus, a love that is so vast and so deep that it led Him to give His life for us.

The spirit of Christmas is not confined to just one day. It extends throughout the season and beyond. December, in particular, is a month where this spirit of giving and kindness seems to flourish. People become more aware of the needs of others, and there is a collective desire to spread joy and generosity. But what if we carried that spirit with us all year long? What if we made paying it forward a daily practice, not just something we do during the holidays?

When we pay it forward, we participate in something larger than ourselves. It's a reminder that we are all connected, that our actions can have a ripple effect, touching lives in ways we may never fully understand. And in doing so, we reflect the heart of Jesus, who gave everything for us.

Christ's life was the ultimate example of selflessness. From the moment He was born, He was destined to give of Himself completely, to lay down His life for the sins of the world. His journey was one of humility and sacrifice, and throughout His ministry, He continually taught the importance of loving others, of putting others before ourselves.

When Jesus washed the feet of His disciples, He was showing them what true leadership and service looked like. He didn't come to be exalted or served; He came to serve others and ultimately to give His life as a ransom for many. This act of washing feet was a profound example of paying it forward—of doing something for someone else, without expectation of repayment. In many ways, every act of kindness we offer is an echo of this moment. When we pay it forward, we are choosing to humble ourselves, to serve others, and to act in love, just as Jesus did.

Paying it forward is also a form of sacrifice. It requires us to step outside of ourselves, to give of our time, our resources, or our attention. And in doing so, we grow in Christ-like character. Sacrifice isn't always about grand gestures; it can be as simple as buying a cup of coffee for someone, giving up our place in line, or offering a word of encouragement. These small acts of love are a reflection of the greater sacrifice that Christ made for us.

Too often, people see Christmas as a single day on the calendar—a day to exchange gifts, eat special meals, and perhaps attend a church service. But Christmas is more than just December 25th. It's a season of reflection and joy that begins long before that day and lingers long after. The spirit of Christmas—one of love, generosity, and kindness—is something we can carry with us throughout the year.

December kicks off this season in a special way. The lights, the music, the gatherings all point to something bigger than the festivities themselves. They point to Jesus. And while Christmas has certainly become commercialized in many ways, its true meaning remains rooted in the love of Christ. This love is what we celebrate, and it's what we are called to share with others. The Christmas season reminds us of the importance of giving—not just material gifts, but the gift of kindness, time, and compassion.

Today, as we begin the countdown to Christmas, let's start by reflecting on the love of Jesus. Let's take time to pray, to commune with God, and to ask Him how we can be a blessing to others during this season. We may not be able to repay Him for all He has done, but we can honor Him by paying it forward, by choosing to give selflessly to those around us.

When we pay it forward, something beautiful happens. Our small act of kindness has the potential to spark a chain reaction of goodness. You never know how your generosity might impact someone's life. Maybe the person you buy coffee for is having a terrible day, and your kindness gives them hope. Maybe paying for someone's groceries lifts a burden they've been carrying in silence. And maybe, just maybe, your act of kindness inspires them to do the same for someone else. This is how the spirit of Christmas spreads—through simple, everyday acts of love.

Paying it forward creates a ripple effect that can extend far beyond what we see or imagine. Each act of kindness is a seed planted, and we may never know the full impact of that seed. But God knows. He sees every small gesture, every act of love, and He uses them to accomplish His purposes in ways we can't always understand.

In a world that often feels disconnected and divided, paying it forward reminds us that we are all part of the same human family. It bridges gaps, heals wounds, and brings light into dark places. And in this way, paying it forward is a reflection of the gospel—the good news of

Jesus Christ, who came to heal, to restore, and to bring light into the darkness of our world.

What if we saw every act of kindness as an act of worship? What if paying it forward became a form of honoring God, of offering up our time and resources as a way to show gratitude for all He has done for us? The Bible tells us that whatever we do for the least of these, we do for Him. When we help others, when we give without expecting anything in return, we are serving Jesus Himself.

As we move through December and the Christmas season, let's make paying it forward part of our worship. Let's look for opportunities to bless others, not just because it feels good, but because it honors God. Whether it's something big or small, every act of kindness is a way of saying, "Thank You, Jesus, for all You've done. I want to share Your love with the world."

Make Something For Someone

I love December, I feel the joy of Christmas spreading even more deeply into my heart and my home. Today, I'm inspired to continue the spirit of Christmas by creating something special for someone else. There's a unique beauty in making something with my own hands, in putting time, thought, and effort into a gift that reflects my love and care. Whether it's baking a batch of warm cookies, cooking up a special dish, or crafting something handmade, this small act of kindness has the power to bring so much joy.

One of the best things about this day's activity is that it's perfect for involving children. If you have little ones, this is an opportunity to teach them about the joy of giving and the delight that comes from sharing something homemade. I've seen firsthand how kids' eyes light up when they hand over a card they drew themselves or present a plate of cookies they helped bake. There's something incredibly precious about letting them experience this—guiding them to understand that the spirit of Christmas is about sharing love and kindness with others. It's a chance for them to see that Christmas isn't only about what they receive, but also about what they can give to others.

With this in mind, I start brainstorming ideas for something I can make. My mind drifts to the smell of gingerbread and sugar cookies, the way the scent fills the house and makes everything feel cozy and warm. I picture little hands helping to roll out dough, adding sprinkles, and carefully placing each cookie on the baking sheet. This simple act, the mixing and shaping, becomes a ritual, a tradition that connects us to the spirit of the season. And when those cookies are finally ready, fresh from the oven, they carry with them more than just their taste—they carry the laughter, the conversations, and the memories we've created along the way.

If baking isn't quite your thing, there are so many other ways to give something handmade. You might decide to make a card, a simple expression of holiday cheer and love that can mean the world to someone. In a time when most of our messages are quick texts or emails, a thoughtful, handwritten card can be a rare and beautiful gesture. It doesn't have to be elaborate or perfect—just a few kind words can be enough to brighten someone's day. If you'd rather go digital, creating an e-card or designing a heartfelt message online can still be just as meaningful, especially for friends and family who are far away. Sometimes, it's these small, thoughtful gestures that make the biggest impact, reminding others that they are loved, valued, and remembered.

And, of course, this day of creativity isn't just about making gifts for others—it's also about the experience itself. Taking the time to slow down, gather supplies, and focus on crafting something from scratch can be a soothing and joyful practice. In the hustle and bustle of December, there's something almost therapeutic about sitting down with a purpose and letting my creativity flow. It's a reminder that Christmas isn't just an event we're rushing toward, but a feeling we can savor in every little moment. And when I involve my children, or even friends and family, it becomes a shared activity that strengthens our bond and creates memories we'll cherish long after the season has passed.

By making something for someone else, we're not only spreading joy, but we're also embracing the spirit of giving that defines Christmas. In the end, it's not about the cookies, the card, or the dish itself—it's about the love and thoughtfulness behind it. When we give something handmade, we're giving a piece of ourselves, showing the other person that they are worth the time, effort, and love we've put into this creation. It's a simple but powerful reminder that the best gifts come from the heart.

As I wrap up my creation, whether it's a warm batch of cookies, a hand-painted card, or a little handmade gift, I'm filled with a sense of peace and fulfillment. I know that what I'm giving is more than just an item—it's a piece of my Christmas spirit, something crafted with love, kindness, and the intention to make someone's day a little brighter. And as I share it, I feel that spirit growing stronger within me, a reminder of why I love this season so much. Christmas is about sharing love, and today, I'm grateful for this simple opportunity to do just that.

There's something truly magical about the act of making something for someone else, and it's more than just the physical creation of a gift—it touches the heart and nourishes the soul in ways that store-bought items never can. When we take the time to put thought and effort into a handmade gift or gesture, it transforms the mundane into something extraordinary. In a world that often feels so self-centered and fast-paced, where we're constantly inundated with messages to think about ourselves first, taking a moment to pause and create something for someone else brings us back to the heart of what matters most: love, kindness, and selflessness.

For me, making something with my hands for another person does more than just fill the recipient with joy—it fills me with a deep sense of fulfillment and peace. Whether I'm cooking a meal for my husband or crafting a small gift for a friend, there's a kind of satisfaction that bubbles up inside me as I think about the happiness my gesture might bring. It's a reminder that the true spirit of giving lies in the act itself—the thought, the effort, and the care we put into it.

Take my husband, for example. Every morning, without fail, he makes me a cup of coffee. Now, I don't drink coffee for the caffeine—no, I drink decaf—but I absolutely adore the smell and taste of it. There's something comforting about holding that warm cup in my hands, inhaling the rich, earthy aroma as I take that first sip. And while I love the coffee, what I love even more is the act behind it. My husband isn't just handing me a cup of coffee—he's offering me a moment of care, a small but powerful expression of his love. Every time he brings me that coffee, I'm reminded of his thoughtfulness, of the way he puts me first, even in such a simple way. It's not about the coffee itself, but the love behind it.

And when I make something for him in return, like his favorite dinner or a special treat, it's a similar experience. I feel a sense of joy and pride in serving him, in knowing that I've created something with my own hands that will bring him happiness. There's an exchange of love that happens when we give to others, especially when that gift is something we've made ourselves. It's not transactional in the way that buying something might feel—there's no price tag, no exchange of goods—but instead, it's an exchange of care and affection. When he praises my cooking or tells me how much he enjoys a meal I've made,

it's like the circle of giving is complete. I've given him something that brings him joy, and in turn, his appreciation and gratitude warm my heart.

Making something for someone else changes the way we think, too. In a world that constantly urges us to think about ourselves—our wants, our needs, our goals—taking the time to create something for someone else shifts our perspective. It pulls us out of the tunnel vision that can sometimes consume our days and reminds us of the importance of others. It reminds us that the most meaningful moments in life often come from putting others before ourselves. In these acts of kindness, we tap into a deeper part of ourselves—the part that is connected to love, compassion, and empathy. And that connection doesn't just benefit the person receiving the gift; it transforms us, too. We become more attuned to the needs of others, more aware of the impact our actions can have, and more grateful for the opportunity to give.

This is especially important in a world that can often feel so selfish. Everywhere we turn, there are messages telling us to prioritize our own success, our own happiness, our own fulfillment. But the truth is, real fulfillment doesn't come from serving ourselves—it comes from serving others. When we step outside of our own desires and focus on the needs or happiness of someone else, we experience a kind of joy that is far more lasting and meaningful than anything we could gain by focusing only on ourselves.

The beauty of making something for someone is that it doesn't have to be grand or complicated. It can be as simple as baking a batch of cookies, knitting a scarf, or writing a heartfelt letter. What matters most is the intention behind it—the thought, the care, and the love that goes into the creation. And when we present that handmade gift to someone, it's not just the physical object we're giving them, but a piece of ourselves. We're offering them our time, our effort, our creativity, and most importantly, our love.

In my own life, I've seen how these small acts of creation can deepen my relationships and strengthen my bonds with the people I care about. When I take the time to make something for someone, I feel more connected to them. I'm not just thinking about myself, but about their happiness, their joy, and how I can contribute to that. And the act of creation itself—whether it's cooking, crafting, or writing—becomes a form of meditation, a way to focus on the person I'm creating for and the love I have for them.

There's also something incredibly freeing about the act of creation. In a world where so much of what we do is dictated by schedules, deadlines, and expectations, making something with our own hands allows us to slow down and engage in a process that is both creative and intentional. We're not rushing through the motions or checking off a to-do list; we're fully present in the act of giving. And that presence is a gift in itself—both for us as the creator and for the person receiving the gift.

On this second day of December, as I think about how to continue spreading the spirit of Christmas, I'm reminded of the power of creation. Today, I challenge myself to make something for someone else—not to buy it, not to take the easy route, but to put in the time and effort to create something that comes from my heart. Whether it's a small batch of cookies, a handmade card, or a simple meal, I know that the act of creating will not only bring joy to the person receiving the gift, but will also warm my own heart in the process.

As I think about what to make, I feel a sense of excitement and anticipation. There's a special kind of magic in knowing that I'm about to give someone something unique, something that no one else could have made in exactly the same way. And as I gather my ingredients, my supplies, or my thoughts, I feel a sense of peace and gratitude for the opportunity to give. Christmas, after all, is about love—and today, I'm choosing to express that love in the most personal way I can, by making something with my own hands.

And when I hand over that gift—whether it's to my husband, my children, a friend, or even a stranger—I know that I'm not just giving them a physical object. I'm giving them a piece of my heart, a symbol of my love, and a reminder that in a world that can often feel rushed and impersonal, there is still space for thoughtfulness, creativity, and care. And that, more than anything, is what the Christmas spirit is all about.

Help Someone

On this beautiful crisp day of December, the air is filled with a crispness that seems to usher in the spirit of the Christmas season. It's the time of year when people bustle about with a different kind of energy—one that hints at generosity, warmth, and togetherness. Christmas lights are starting to blink on porches and rooftops, and the scent of pine trees and cinnamon seems to float through the air. I find myself reflecting on the true meaning of the season, not just the outward festivities, but the essence of giving—selflessly, without expectation. I have always believed that Christmas is more than a day, it's a mindset, a way of being, and an opportunity to mirror Christ's love through our actions.

This morning, I received an unexpected opportunity to help someone with a small but meaningful task. As I was leaving my house, I noticed my elderly neighbor, Mrs. Jenkins, struggling to wheel her trash can back up the driveway. She's in her late seventies, and even though she still tries to do everything on her own, I've seen how age has slowed her down over the years. Her hands shook slightly as she gripped the handle of the trash bin, her pace slow and unsteady. Normally, I might give a quick wave or smile in passing, but something inside me nudged me to stop. It was a small moment, but one that seemed to be wrapped in the meaning of the season—a chance to serve without being asked.

"Let me help you with that, Mrs. Jenkins," I called out as I crossed the street. Her face lit up in surprise, and then a warm smile spread across her face.

"Oh, bless your heart! These old bones just aren't what they used to be," she chuckled, stepping aside as I took the handle from her hands.

It was such a simple act, something I could have easily overlooked, but as I guided the trash can back to her garage, I realized how much these little things mean. For Mrs. Jenkins, it wasn't just about the task itself—it was the gesture, the acknowledgment that someone cared enough to take a moment from their busy day to lend a hand. We chatted for a few minutes as I walked back, talking about her Christmas plans and how she used to host family dinners for her children and grandchildren. But now, with most of her family living far away, the holidays had grown quieter for her. She didn't say it, but I could sense a loneliness that sometimes settles in during this time of year, especially for those who no longer have their loved ones close by.

As I returned home, I felt a warmth that had nothing to do with the chill in the air or the season itself. It was the realization that, in some small way, I had brightened her day. In the grand scheme of things, it didn't feel like much, but isn't that what Christmas is about? It's not always about grand gestures or expensive gifts, but rather the small acts of kindness that ripple outwards, creating a sense of community and love. Christ's life was filled with moments like these—helping others, lifting burdens, showing love and compassion to the people around Him. And today, on the third day of December, I was reminded that the best way to celebrate His birth is by doing the same.

Later that day, I found myself thinking about other ways I could help people this month, even if it was just something small. I decided to keep an eye out for opportunities, whether it was bringing in a co-worker's lunch from their car, holding the door open for a stranger, or simply listening to someone who needed to talk. Every task, every moment of service, no matter how trivial it might seem, is an offering—an acknowledgment that we are all connected and that the love of Christ flows through us when we give of ourselves to others.

As we journey through the rest of this month, leading up to the celebration of Christ's birth, I'm reminded that Christmas is not just a time to receive but also a time to give. And not just gifts wrapped in bows and ribbons, but the kind of giving that speaks to the heart—acts of kindness, moments of service, and gestures that say, "I see you, and I care." Helping Mrs. Jenkins today was a simple task, but it was one of many opportunities to embody the spirit of Christmas in a real and meaningful way. The season is rich with these moments, and I'm grateful for the chance to be part of them.

When we help others, we become a reflection of God's love, a vessel through which His grace, mercy, and compassion can flow into the world. In the simplest of acts, we participate in something far greater than ourselves—an eternal cycle of giving that mirrors the very heart of Christ. Jesus' life was built upon helping others, and He repeatedly emphasized the importance of serving those in need. One of the most profound scriptures that speaks to the heart of helping others comes from Matthew 25:40 (NIV): "The King will reply, 'Truly I tell you, whatever you did for one of the least of these brothers and sisters of mine, you did for me.'"

This verse encapsulates the idea that when we help others, we are, in fact, serving Christ Himself. Every time we lend a hand to someone in need, offer a word of comfort, or share our resources with those less fortunate, we are fulfilling one of God's greatest commandments: to love our neighbors as ourselves. It's a powerful realization, that the small, everyday acts of kindness we perform are deeply significant in the eyes of God. Through these actions, we demonstrate our faith, not just with words, but with deeds.

In the book of Galatians 6:2 (NIV), Paul writes, "Carry each other's burdens, and in this way, you will fulfill the law of Christ." Helping others is not just a recommendation, it is a calling. We are called to walk alongside one another in times of need, to share in the trials and tribulations of our brothers and sisters. When we take on someone else's burden, whether physical, emotional, or spiritual, we lighten their load and bring them closer to the peace that God desires for all of us.

This concept is also echoed in Philippians 2:4 (NIV): "Each of you should look not only to your own interests, but also to the interests of others." We live in a world that often prioritizes individualism and personal gain, but as

Christians, we are called to be countercultural. Helping others requires us to shift our focus from ourselves to the needs of those around us. It's an act of humility, o recognizing that we are all interconnected and that ou purpose is fulfilled not through selfish ambition, but throug service.

When we help others, something transformative happens within us as well. It softens our hearts, increases our empathy, and brings us closer to God. Acts 20:35 (NIV) reminds us, "It is more blessed to give than to receive." There is a unique joy that comes from helping others, a deep, spiritual fulfillment that cannot be replicated. Helping others is so rewarding.

Puzzle Swap

I woke up with a burst of inspiration for a festive activity that could bring my friends and family together: a Christmas puzzle swap. The idea blossomed in my mind as I sipped my morning coffee, watching the soft glow of twinkling lights on the tree. Puzzles have always held a special place in my heart, serving as a perfect blend of challenge and relaxation, and I thought, what better way to foster connection and create joy during this holiday season than by sharing something so wholesome?

As I contemplated the logistics, I envisioned inviting a group of my closest friends and family over for an afternoon filled with laughter, chatter, and the delightful clinking of hot cocoa mugs. I decided to send out a fun invitation that captured the spirit of the event: "Join us for a Christmas Puzzle Swap! Bring a holiday-themed puzzle you've completed and get ready to trade for a new one! Let's enjoy the warmth of the season together as we sip cocoa, nibble on cookies, and piece together memories." I hoped the theme would add a playful twist, making everyone feel the anticipation of not only exchanging puzzles but also diving into the holiday spirit.

In preparation, I rummaged through my collection of puzzles, eager to select one that had bright, festive artwork. I found a beautifully illustrated scene of a bustling winter village, with children playing in the snow and twinkling lights adorning cozy cottages. It reminded me of childhood days spent huddled indoors with family, piecing together puzzles while the snow fell outside. I felt a pang of nostalgia, knowing this particular puzzle would bring a smile to someone else's face just as it had to mine.

As the day of the swap approached, I could hardly contain my excitement. I decided to prepare a cozy atmosphere in my living room, with blankets draped over the couches and tables adorned with holiday decorations. I set out trays of cookies—gingerbread men, peppermint bark, and sugar cookies frosted with vibrant colors—and brewed a big pot of hot cocoa, complete with whipped cream and candy canes for garnish. I wanted everyone to feel welcome and to embrace the joy of the season.

When the day arrived, I greeted my guests at the door, their arms laden with wrapped puzzles, each bearing unique stories and memories. The laughter and chatter filled my home as we settled into the living room, everyone eager to share their puzzle experiences. Some had spent countless evenings assembling intricate designs, while others had just completed their first holiday puzzle. Each story added a layer of connection, turning the event into a delightful exchange of not just puzzles but also shared experiences and joy.

Once everyone was settled, I explained the rules of the swap. We would take turns sharing our puzzles, explaining what drew us to them, and then we'd draw numbers to determine the order of selection. As we began, I watched as eyes lit up with excitement. Friends and family exchanged puzzled looks of anticipation as they listened to each person share about their chosen puzzle. I could feel the festive spirit wrapping around us like a warm blanket, drawing us closer together in that cozy atmosphere.

The moment of the swap was filled with joyous banter, laughter, and friendly competition. As people selected their new puzzles, they couldn't help but share ideas about which ones would be fun to tackle together. It was heartwarming to witness how excited everyone became about trying something new, the spirit of giving intertwining with the joy of receiving. We even set aside time for a mini-puzzle competition, where pairs teamed up to race against the clock to complete a holiday puzzle in record time. It was a lighthearted, spirited challenge that had everyone in stitches.

The day rolled on with snacks being devoured, cocoa cups refilled, and friends sharing more stories and memories than I could have anticipated. I felt a sense of warmth enveloping us—a reminder of why this season is so special. It wasn't just about the puzzles; it was about the connections we were fostering and the memories we were creating together. I realized how significant such gatherings are, especially during a time when life can feel hectic and overwhelming.

As the afternoon turned to evening, the last of the cookies were consumed, and we wrapped up the event by each taking a moment to express gratitude for our friendships and the joy of the season. I reflected on how this simple idea had transformed into something more meaningful, a celebration of community, warmth, and the spirit of Christmas. Each puzzle would now carry not only its own challenge but also the stories of the people who exchanged them—stories filled with laughter, nostalgia, and love.

As everyone departed with their new puzzles in hand, I couldn't help but feel a swell of joy and contentment. This was the magic of Christmas—the connections we build, the love we share, and the way simple ideas can blossom into cherished traditions. I was grateful for the laughter and love shared in my home that day, and I vowed to make the Christmas puzzle swap an annual tradition, a beloved reminder that the spirit of Christmas shines brightest when we come together to share our joy with one another.

The Christmas puzzle swap I organized blossomed into more than just a fun activity; it became a heartfelt gathering that exemplified the true spirit of the season, bringing friends and family closer together in ways I hadn't anticipated. As the day unfolded, I was reminded of how something as simple as sharing a puzzle could weave

deeper connections and create lasting memories, all while embracing the themes of love, generosity, and togetherness that define Christmas.

The preparation for the puzzle swap was filled with excitement, but it was the anticipation of gathering everyone that truly made my heart swell. I carefully crafted the invitation, hoping to convey the warmth and joy that the holiday season embodies. As friends and family arrived, I was struck by the sense of familiarity and warmth that filled the room. It was as if the spirit of Christmas had wrapped itself around us, inviting us to slow down and savor each moment.

The décor contributed significantly to the atmosphere. I adorned my living room with twinkling lights, vibrant wreaths, and festive ornaments, creating a cozy ambiance that encouraged connection. The aroma of freshly baked cookies and the sweet scent of hot cocoa wafted through the air, making everyone feel instantly at home. As guests settled in, the laughter and chatter began, creating a joyful symphony that filled the space with love.

As each person shared the story behind their chosen puzzle, I was struck by the richness of our collective experiences. Some puzzles represented cherished family traditions, handed down through generations, while others were newfound treasures discovered in quaint shops. The act of sharing these stories not only highlighted the individuality of each puzzle but also showcased the unique tapestry of our friendships and family ties.

One friend recounted how she and her grandmother used to spend rainy afternoons assembling puzzles, creating a bond that transcended generations. Another shared his excitement about a complex winter scene he had tackled with his children, emphasizing the joy of family bonding during the holiday season. As we listened, we found ourselves reminiscing about our own experiences—nostalgic moments spent piecing together puzzles with loved ones, all of which reinforced the sense of community and shared history we had built over the years.

The heart of the puzzle swap was not just in the exchange of puzzles but in the act of giving and receiving. Each person brought a puzzle they had enjoyed, filled with memories and challenges, and as they gifted it to someone else, they were also sharing a piece of their holiday spirit. The excitement of selecting a new puzzle added an element of surprise, enhancing the joy of the event.

During the swap, I noticed how the act of giving sparked genuine happiness in each participant. Faces lit up as friends chose puzzles that resonated with them, and the heartfelt gratitude exchanged felt almost palpable. This exchange embodied the essence of Christmas, a time when we come together to celebrate not only what we have but also what we can share with others.

As we delved into the swapping process, the atmosphere became electric with playful competition. Teams formed for mini-puzzle challenges, laughter erupting as we raced to complete holiday-themed puzzles. This lighthearted activity broke down barriers and encouraged everyone to engage with one another, fostering a sense of camaraderie and teamwork.

Through these shared experiences, friendships were strengthened and new bonds formed. People who had previously been acquaintances found common ground as they teamed up, exchanging tips and strategies to tackle the puzzles. In this way, the puzzle swap became a catalyst for deeper connections, reminding us that the spirit of Christmas thrives when we unite in joy and laughter.

As the evening progressed, it became evident that this gathering was creating lasting memories that would be cherished long after the holiday season. We took photos, capturing the joy of the moment, and I encouraged everyone to share their experiences on social media, creating a digital scrapbook of our time together. Each puzzle would now carry a story—an imprint of laughter, joy, and shared experiences, transforming them into cherished keepsakes.

Reflecting on the event, I realized how important it is to create opportunities for connection during the holiday season. In our fast-paced lives, it's easy to lose sight of what truly matters: the relationships we cultivate and the love we share. The puzzle swap not only brought friends and family together but also served as a reminder to pause, appreciate, and celebrate our connections.

Ultimately, the Christmas puzzle swap exemplified the true spirit of the season. It was about more than just puzzles; it was about love, community, and the joy of coming together. As we exchanged laughter and stories, we were reminded of the values that Christmas embodies—generosity, kindness, and togetherness.

As I reflected on the day, I felt immense gratitude for the friendships in my life and the opportunity to share such a special occasion with the people I love. The warmth that enveloped us was a testament to the power of connection, a reminder that in helping others find joy and creating opportunities for togetherness, we keep the spirit of Christmas alive.

As we embraced the holiday season, I knew that this puzzle swap would become a cherished tradition, a yearly celebration of friendship and community that would continue to grow and evolve. With each passing year, I looked forward to the new stories that would unfold, the laughter that would fill my home, and the spirit of Christmas that would shine brighter than ever, brought to life through the simple yet profound act of sharing puzzles and creating memories together.

Volunteer At A Shelter or Food Bank

On a brisk December morning, I awoke with a sense of excitement bubbling within me. I had planned a special day with my husband, Jeff. We had both agreed that this year, we wanted to immerse ourselves in the true spirit of Christmas—not just in our own home but within our community. We were eager to give back and share our blessings with others. As I sipped my morning coffee, I felt a warm anticipation, knowing this day would be memorable.

Jeff and I had chosen to volunteer at a local shelter, a place that provided meals and support to those in need. We had discussed this idea for weeks, and today was finally the day. After a quick breakfast and some final preparations, we bundled up in cozy clothes and made our way to the shelter. The drive through the city was filled with animated chatter as we reminisced about past holiday seasons and shared our hopes for this one. We talked about how, sometimes, the best way to celebrate is to step outside our own lives and help those who might be struggling, especially during the holidays.

When we arrived at the shelter, the atmosphere buzzed with activity. Volunteers bustled about, and the scent of delicious food wafted from the kitchen, mingling with laughter and conversations. Jeff and I were greeted warmly by the volunteer coordinator, who quickly guided us to our tasks for the day. We were assigned to help serve lunch, and I felt a rush of excitement as we gathered in the kitchen, ready to dive into our work.

Working side by side with Jeff made the experience even more special. We chopped vegetables together, mixed ingredients, and prepared trays of hearty soup and sandwiches. As we worked, we exchanged smiles and quick jokes, our laughter blending harmoniously with the sounds of the bustling kitchen. It was a beautiful reminder of how even the simplest tasks become meaningful when shared with someone you love.

Once the food was prepared and the tables set, the moment we had been eagerly anticipating arrived. The doors of the shelter opened, and the first guests began to enter. Jeff and I took our positions at the serving line, and I watched as he greeted each person with a warm smile, his kindness shining through. We served meal after meal, filling plates with hearty portions and offering warm bread on the side. Each time a guest expressed their gratitude, I could see the joy in Jeff's eyes; it was evident that we were both touched by this experience.

As we served, I noticed the diversity among the guests—individuals from various backgrounds and ages, each with their own stories. I marveled at how this simple act of sharing food could create a sense of community and connection. Jeff and I engaged in conversations with the guests, asking how their day was going and listening intently to their stories. One elderly gentleman shared tales of his life and his love for cooking, which sparked a lively discussion about favorite holiday recipes. Jeff and I exchanged knowing glances, reveling in the warmth that filled the room.

After we served lunch, we moved around the shelter, helping guests find seats and offering them beverages. I was struck by the way the shelter buzzed with energy, laughter, and shared experiences. People who often felt isolated were coming together in this space, united by the common bond of humanity. As Jeff and I interacted with everyone, I felt the spirit of Christmas envelop us—a spirit of giving, compassion, and connection.

After the meal, we helped clean up, continuing our conversations and laughter with both the guests and fellow volunteers. Jeff shared a story about our family Christmas traditions, and the guests responded with their own anecdotes. It was a beautiful exchange of experiences, each story woven into the fabric of our shared humanity. Throughout the day, I could feel the weight of the world lifting from my shoulders. I had entered the shelter wanting to help others, but I found myself nourished by the very act of service. Jeff and I shared glances filled with understanding—this was more than just a task; it was a meaningful way to celebrate the holiday season.

As the afternoon drew to a close, Jeff and I stepped outside to take a breath of fresh air. The sun was beginning to set, painting the sky with hues of pink and orange. I turned to him, my heart full. "Today was incredible," I said, feeling the warmth of gratitude wash over me. Jeff nodded in agreement, his eyes shining with the same joy I felt. "It's amazing how much we can learn from those we aim to help. I think we're the ones who ended up being blessed."

On our drive home, the conversation flowed effortlessly as we reflected on the day's events. We talked about the stories we had heard, the smiles we had exchanged, and the sense of community that had enveloped us. I realized how volunteering together had strengthened our bond, allowing us to share a deeper understanding of what it means to give selflessly.

That evening, as we settled in for a cozy night at home, I felt an overwhelming sense of peace. We decorated our Christmas tree, hanging ornaments that held memories of years past. The twinkling lights reflected the joy in our hearts, reminding us that the true spirit of Christmas is not found in material gifts but in the connections we create and the love we share.

As we prepared for bed, I reflected on our day—the laughter, the kindness, and the shared experiences that had touched our souls. I felt grateful for Jeff, for our shared commitment to serving others, and for the countless blessings in our lives. In those moments of gratitude, I knew that the spirit of Christmas would continue to guide us in our journey together, inspiring us to keep giving and loving long after the holiday season had passed.

As we settled into the warmth of our home after a fulfilling day of service, my thoughts turned to the scriptures that remind us of the importance of serving others, especially during the Christmas season. The Bible is rich with teachings that emphasize compassion, kindness, and the call to support those in need, echoing the very essence of the Christmas spirit.

One of the passages that resonated deeply with me was found in Matthew 25:35-40 (NIV), where Jesus shares a powerful message about serving others. He states, "For I was hungry and you gave me something to eat, I was thirsty and you gave me something to drink, I was a stranger and you invited me in, I needed clothes and you clothed me, I was sick and you looked after me, I was in prison and you came to visit me." The scripture continues, with Jesus explaining that whatever we do for the least of our brothers and sisters, we do for Him. This teaching encapsulates the spirit of Christmas—serving those in need as an act of love and reverence for Christ.

Reflecting on this scripture, I recognized that Christmas is more than just a celebration of Christ's birth; it's an invitation to embody His teachings of love and service. Every act of kindness, whether it's serving a meal at a shelter or lending a hand to a neighbor, becomes a testament to our faith and a way to honor His presence in our lives. In times of need, we can be the hands and feet of Christ, spreading joy and compassion in a world that sometimes feels heavy with burdens.

Another powerful verse is found in Galatians 6:2 (NIV): "Carry each other's burdens, and in this way, you will fulfill the law of Christ." This scripture emphasizes the communal nature of our faith and the call to support one another. During the holiday season, many people experience loneliness, grief, and hardship, making it all the more important for us to reach out and offer our help. Whether it's through volunteering, providing a meal, or simply offering a listening ear, each act of service helps lighten the load for those around us.

As Jeff and I reflected on our day of service, I felt inspired to keep this scripture in mind. Each moment spent helping others felt like fulfilling a sacred duty—one that not only aided those in need but also enriched our own hearts. We were reminded that service is a two-way street: while we help carry the burdens of others, we, too, receive the gift of connection, love, and fulfillment.

In James 2:14-17 (NIV), we are reminded of the necessity of action alongside our faith. The passage reads, "What good is it, my brothers and sisters, if someone claims to have faith but has no deeds? Can such faith save them? Suppose a brother or sister is without clothes and daily food. If one of you says to them, 'Go in peace; keep warm and well fed,' but does nothing about their physical needs, what good is it?" This scripture powerfully illustrates that true faith is demonstrated through our actions. As we celebrate Christmas, we can embody this message by taking tangible steps to support those around us.

Christmas gives us an opportunity to reflect on how we can serve others more intentionally. It encourages us to reach out and provide for those who are struggling, just as we would hope others would do for us. With each act of kindness, we honor the spirit of Christmas and the message of hope that Christ brings into the world.

Lastly, I think of Philippians 2:3-4 (NIV), which encourages us to "Do nothing out of selfish ambition or vain conceit. Rather, in humility value others above yourselves, not looking to your own interests but each of you to the interests of the others." This call to humility and selflessness serves as a guiding principle for our actions, especially during the Christmas season. It challenges us to shift our focus from ourselves to those around us, fostering an environment of compassion and generosity.

As I sit here reflecting on the day and the scriptures that encourage us to serve others, I feel a renewed sense of purpose. Christmas is a time to extend grace, love, and support, not just to our loved ones but to everyone within our reach. It's about embracing the true essence of the holiday by opening our hearts and hands to those in need.

In our journey through life, especially during this season of celebration, let us remember to serve others with love and humility. Each act of kindness is a reflection of our faith and a way to share the joy of Christ's birth with the world. As we continue to celebrate this holiday season, I am committed to seeking out opportunities to serve and uplift others, knowing that in doing so, we truly embody the spirit of Christmas.

Create Care Packages For The Homeless

As I reflected on the day spent creating care packages for the homeless, I was reminded of the profound biblical teachings that emphasize the importance of serving those in need. The Scriptures resonate deeply with the values of compassion and generosity, especially during the Christmas season when we celebrate the ultimate gift of love through Christ. One verse that stood out to me was found in the Gospel of Matthew: "For I was hungry and you gave me something to eat, I was thirsty and you gave me something to drink, I was a stranger and you invited me in" (Matthew 25:35, NIV). This verse captures the essence of what it means to serve others, reminding us that our actions toward those in need are a reflection of our faith.

As Jeff and I engaged in our day of service, I couldn't help but feel a deep connection to this scripture. Each care package we assembled was a response to that call, a tangible expression of love for those who may feel forgotten or marginalized. It became clear to me that in serving the homeless, we were not only meeting their physical needs but also honoring the divine mandate to love our neighbors as ourselves. This sentiment echoes through the Bible in various passages, urging us to remember those who are less fortunate.

Another verse that resonated profoundly was found in the book of Proverbs: "Whoever is generous to the poor lends to the Lord, and he will repay him for his deed" (Proverbs 19:17, ESV). This scripture emphasizes the notion that when we extend our hands to help those in need, we are, in essence, lending to God Himself. It fills my heart with hope to know that our efforts, no matter how small, are valued and rewarded by the Almighty. As we handed out the care packages, I felt a sense of divine purpose guiding us, knowing that our actions were aligning with God's will for compassion and generosity.

I also found encouragement in the book of Isaiah, which speaks to the heart of God's desire for justice and mercy: "Is not this the kind of fasting I have chosen: to loose the chains of injustice and untie the cords of the yoke, to set the oppressed free and break every yoke?" (Isaiah 58:6, NIV). This verse challenges us to look

beyond our personal needs and comforts and to engage actively in acts of justice. It reminds me that the Christmas season is not merely about celebration but also about recognizing the plight of the oppressed and working toward their liberation.

In our modern world, the challenges faced by the homeless and needy can sometimes feel overwhelming. However, the Bible encourages us not to lose heart. In Galatians, we read: "Let us not become weary in doing good, for at the proper time we will reap a harvest if we do not give up" (Galatians 6:9, NIV). This verse serves as a powerful reminder that every act of kindness, no matter how small, contributes to a greater tapestry of hope and love. It urges me to keep pressing on, especially during the holiday season when many may feel discouraged or forgotten.

During our time distributing care packages, I felt an overwhelming sense of joy as we connected with individuals who expressed gratitude for our presence and generosity. One woman, her face lighting up with surprise

as she received a warm pair of socks, said, "You have no idea how much this means to me." In that moment, I was reminded of the words of James: "Religion that God our Father accepts as pure and faultless is this: to look after orphans and widows in their distress and to keep oneself from being polluted by the world" (James 1:27, NIV). It became clear to me that our efforts to help

those in need were a reflection of our faith and a call to action that resonates throughout the Bible.

As I continued to reflect on the Scriptures that guide us in serving others, I thought about the parable of the Good Samaritan found in Luke 10:25-37. In this story, Jesus teaches us about the true nature of love and compassion through the actions of the Samaritan who, despite cultural boundaries, stopped to help a wounded stranger. Jesus concludes the parable by saying, "Go and do likewise" (Luke 10:37, NIV). This message is clear: we are called to act with kindness and mercy, to reach out to those in need, and to be the hands and feet of Jesus in a world that desperately requires His love.

In my heart, I felt a growing desire to embrace this call not just during the Christmas season but as a continual lifestyle choice. As Jeff and I discussed the day's events, we recognized the profound impact that simple acts of kindness can have on individuals and communities. We were reminded of the words of Jesus in John: "By this everyone will know that you are my disciples if you love one another" (John 13:35, NIV). Our commitment to serving others is not just an isolated act; it is a testament to our faith and the transformative power of love.

As December unfolds, I am increasingly aware of the importance of keeping our focus on the true meaning of Christmas. The holiday season can easily become consumed by materialism and busyness, but the Scriptures continually call us back to a life of service and generosity. I reflect on the words of 1 John: "Dear children, let us not love with words or speech but with actions and in truth" (1 John 3:18, NIV). This verse challenges me to embody love in practical ways, to seek out opportunities to serve, and to demonstrate compassion that goes beyond mere words.

Throughout our day of service, I felt my heart expanding with each connection we made. The faces of those we encountered, each with their unique story and struggle, served as a poignant reminder of our shared humanity. In the book of Matthew, we are reminded that our actions toward the least among us are, in fact, actions toward Christ Himself: "Truly I tell you, whatever you did for one of the least of these brothers and sisters of mine, you did for me" (Matthew 25:40, NIV). This understanding deepens my motivation to serve, knowing that every act of kindness carries eternal significance.

As I look forward to the days ahead, I am filled with anticipation for the opportunities that await us. I want to encourage Jeff and me, as well as our friends and family, to keep our eyes open to those around us who may be in need. The Christmas spirit is alive in acts of service, and the Scriptures remind us that we have the power to bring hope, joy, and love into the lives of others.

Through my journey of creating care packages, I have grown more aware of the importance of intentionality in our service. It's not enough to simply want to help; we must actively seek ways to engage with those in need. In Proverbs, we are reminded that "The generous will themselves be blessed, for they share their food with the poor" (Proverbs 22:9, NIV). This commitment to generosity fosters a spirit of gratitude within us, reminding us of the abundance we possess and the responsibility we have to share it with others.

As we continue this journey through December, I am reminded of the beautiful call to serve those in need. The Scriptures are rich with teachings that urge us to care for the homeless, the hungry, and the marginalized. Each verse resonates deeply within me, igniting a passion to embody love in tangible ways. I am excited to embrace the spirit of Christmas through acts of service, knowing that each small contribution can create ripples of hope and joy in the world around us. Together with Jeff, I look forward to continuing this journey, fueled by the love of Christ and a desire to make a meaningful difference in the lives of others.

Host A Holiday Movie Night

The spirit of Christmas filled our home as Jeff and I decided to host a holiday movie night, inviting family and close friends over for a cozy evening of togetherness. The idea of gathering everyone under one roof, surrounded by twinkling lights, Christmas decorations, and the warmth of the fireplace, felt perfectly in line with the season. There's something magical about the power of a good holiday film to bring people together, drawing out laughter, nostalgia, and even a few joyful tears. Christmas movies have a way of making us feel closer, of reminding us of the simple beauty of the season and the timeless messages of love, kindness, and generosity.

From the moment we decided to plan this night, excitement filled every part of the process. I could already imagine the aroma of freshly popped popcorn and the rich, comforting scent of hot cocoa wafting through the air. Jeff and I carefully chose a selection of Christmas classics that would capture the hearts of everyone, from the younger ones to the older guests who held childhood memories of these films. We wanted this night to not only be about watching movies but also to be an experience that embraced the essence of the season—a night that would leave each guest feeling warmed by the Christmas spirit.

As the day drew closer, I spent time decorating our living room, transforming it into a festive wonderland. Soft, fuzzy blankets were draped across every sofa and chair, and pillows in reds, greens, and golds added to the Christmas charm. I adorned our walls with string lights that twinkled like stars, and a soft glow from candles created a welcoming atmosphere. The Christmas tree, proudly standing in the corner, sparkled with lights and ornaments, radiating a feeling of joy and wonder. This holiday movie night wasn't just about watching films—it was about creating an environment where everyone felt cherished, safe, and embraced by the spirit of the season.

On the night of our gathering, friends and family arrived, bundled up in winter coats, scarves, and mittens, their cheeks flushed from the cold air outside. As they stepped into our home, greeted by the scent of cinnamon and pine, their faces lit up with excitement. We shared warm hugs, laughter, and stories as everyone settled in, filling the room with a wonderful buzz of anticipation. It felt like a scene from one of those Christmas movies, where the holiday magic is real and alive, surrounding everyone with warmth and joy.

We started the evening with one of my favorite Christmas classics, a film that brought out the innocence and wonder of the holiday. As the movie played, I watched the faces of our friends and family members, each person engaged in their own way. Some of them were laughing, others had soft, thoughtful smiles, and a few were even misty-eyed during the heartfelt moments. It reminded me of how powerful these stories are—they bring out emotions that connect us and, even more so, remind us of what truly matters during the holiday season. The beauty of hosting this movie night lay in the simple, shared experience of laughter, reflection, and the warmth of being together.

Jeff and I made sure everyone had their hands wrapped around warm mugs of cocoa, complete with fluffy marshmallows and a hint of cinnamon. The richness of the hot chocolate combined with the aroma of freshly popped popcorn created a nostalgic ambiance that seemed to fill the room with memories of Christmases past. I noticed some of our friends glancing at the decorations around the room, reminiscing about similar decorations in their childhood homes. The holiday season has a way of reminding us of where we came from and the little traditions that brought us joy in our younger years.

Between movies, we'd pause to chat, sharing memories and holiday plans, swapping stories of past Christmases and the funny or sentimental things we each remembered.

Someone would recall a Christmas morning when they stayed up all night in excitement, while another would talk about baking cookies with their grandmother. These moments, woven in between our films, filled the night with a warmth that only Christmas could bring.

One of the movies we chose was a timeless classic that spoke of selflessness, love, and the value of family and friendship. Watching it as a group allowed us to experience the themes of the film in a way that felt real and personal. As scenes unfolded on the screen, I felt a renewed sense of gratitude for everyone in the room, for the bonds we shared, and for the simple fact that we could come together and celebrate in this way. Jeff gave my hand a gentle squeeze, as if to say he felt the same. There's something beautiful about how Christmas movies can stir up these deep feelings, making us realize that we are part of something greater—a family, a community, a shared experience.

As the night went on, we wrapped up our movie lineup with a heartwarming comedy that had everyone laughing. Laughter filled the room, echoing off the walls and mixing with the crackling of the fire. It was the kind of laughter that leaves your heart feeling light and your spirit lifted. I could feel that everyone was enjoying the pure, unfiltered joy of being together, and it reminded me that the essence of Christmas is found in these simple, heartfelt moments.

Finally, as the night drew to a close, we exchanged warm goodbyes and hugs, with everyone expressing their thanks for the evening. I could see the contentment on their faces as they left, bundled up once more to brave the chilly December air. Jeff and I stood by the door, watching them leave with hearts full of gratitude. We knew that this holiday movie night had been more than just an evening of watching films; it had been a time to reconnect, to share love and laughter, and to bask in the glow of the Christmas spirit.

After everyone left, Jeff and I sat together, reflecting on the night. We talked about how wonderful it was to bring everyone together, to laugh, to remember, and to celebrate the season in such a simple yet meaningful way. Hosting this holiday movie night had reminded us both of the true spirit of Christmas—of sharing, of giving, and of being fully present with those we love. We felt blessed to have been able to open our home and create a space where everyone could feel the joy and warmth of the season.

As we finally turned off the lights and made our way to bed, I knew that the memory of this night would stay with us for a long time. It was a reminder that sometimes, the greatest gift we can give is simply our time and presence. In the days that followed, we continued to feel the warmth of that night, carrying the joy of togetherness with us as we moved through the rest of December. Hosting a holiday movie night had not only brought our friends and family together but had also deepened our own appreciation for the magic of Christmas and the beauty of being surrounded by loved ones.

And so, on that seventh day of December, our home was filled with laughter, warmth, and the spirit of Christmas—a spirit that lingered in our hearts, reminding us of the importance of gathering, of sharing love, and of creating memories that would last far beyond the holiday season.

For our holiday movie night, Jeff and I decided on a theme that went beyond traditional Christmas classics; we chose to focus on films that celebrated the true spirit of Christmas and the values of Christ. With careful thought, we selected a lineup of movies that shared messages of kindness, redemption, sacrifice, and the boundless love that aligns so closely with the teachings of Jesus. From tales of generosity and second chances to stories of unconditional love and selflessness, our movie theme would reflect what Christmas is truly about: celebrating Christ's love through our lives and actions.

As I prepared the living room, thoughts filled my mind about how powerful movies could be in conveying the heart of Christmas. There's something profound about watching a story unfold on screen, seeing characters

struggle with doubt, fear, or loneliness, only to discover the light of love and hope. I knew that choosing a Christ-centered movie theme would allow us all to reflect on our own lives and inspire us to live out the messages of the season beyond the holiday. We aimed to create a meaningful experience for everyone who would join us that evening.

Our movie night began with a film that carried a message of forgiveness and second chances, a theme that resonates so deeply with the teachings of Christ. I looked around the room as our guests were drawn into the story, their expressions revealing moments of thoughtfulness and connection. Forgiveness is a cornerstone of the Christmas message—Jesus came into the world to offer forgiveness, to mend broken lives and bring hope to the hopeless. As we watched, I felt a sense of peace, knowing that this story could touch the hearts of everyone present, reminding us of the grace we've each been shown and the grace we're called to extend to others.

Between films, Jeff and I served warm cups of spiced cider and set out trays of treats, creating a cozy space for conversation. We took this time to share our own stories and discuss what forgiveness and second chances have meant to each of us. It was beautiful to see everyone open up, sharing their thoughts and experiences, connecting over themes that were both universal and deeply personal.

Conversations flowed naturally, and I could see how much this Christ-centered theme was resonating with each person, sparking reflection on how we might live these principles in our own lives.

The next film was a heartwarming story about a community that came together to help those in need, an inspiring reminder of the Christmas spirit of generosity and giving. As we watched, Jeff leaned over to me and whispered how much he appreciated the reminder of how Christ gave freely and selflessly, not just on Christmas but throughout His life. Watching this story unfold on screen encouraged us to think about the ways we could be more giving, more willing to lend a hand, and more open to sharing what we have with others. I could feel the warmth of love and compassion filling the room, touching each person in its own unique way.

Once the movie ended, we began talking about the ways we could put this spirit into action. Someone shared an idea of organizing a Christmas drive to gather food, clothing, and blankets for those who might be struggling during the holiday season. Another friend talked about visiting a local nursing home to bring gifts and spend time with the residents who might feel lonely. It was amazing to see how the movie had sparked such tangible ideas for making a difference in the lives of others. In that moment, it became clear that our movie night was becoming more than just an evening of entertainment; it was planting seeds of love, kindness, and generosity.

We ended our night with a classic film that captured the joy of finding light in the darkness—a message that speaks directly to the hope Jesus brought into the world. Christmas is, after all, a celebration of the Light that came into a dark world, a reminder that even in our hardest moments, there is always hope. Watching this movie with our friends and family felt like a powerful way to end the evening, a reminder to carry the light of Christ with us and to share it with others. As the movie closed, I felt a sense of deep contentment, knowing that the night had left a meaningful impression on each of us.

Gathered together, our hearts full and our spirits lifted, we said our goodbyes, exchanging hugs and words of gratitude for the experience we'd shared. Watching films that celebrated the teachings of Christ, and then discussing them together, had brought us all closer, strengthening the bonds of friendship and family. As Jeff and I cleaned up, we talked about how rewarding it was to share this Christ-centered movie night with those we love. It reminded us that the spirit of Christmas isn't something that can be contained in a single day or a single gathering—it's a way of life, a commitment to love, serve, and spread hope wherever we go.

Through that one night of movies and conversations, we were reminded of the richness of Christmas, the joy of connecting with loved ones, and the deep satisfaction that comes from centering our celebrations around the love of Christ. As we reflected on the night, we both felt inspired to continue finding ways to spread the spirit of Christmas in our daily lives, knowing that the impact of these small acts of kindness, forgiveness, and love can reach far beyond the holiday season. In the end, the true blessing of our holiday movie night was discovering how the spirit of Christmas could live on in our hearts and actions long after the decorations were packed away and the last Christmas lights turned off.

Holiday Book Drive

Jeff and I decided to organize a holiday book drive, a mission near and dear to my heart. By the grace of God, I've been blessed to write 100 books, including more than 85 for children and 15 for adults across various genres. Writing has always been my passion, and it's both humbling and thrilling to see how God has used this gift to inspire, teach, and bring joy to others. Over the years, Jeff and I have grown to love organizing book drives, especially during the holiday season when the spirit of

Christmas is all around us, and there's a certain magic that fills the air.

There's something profoundly rewarding about knowing each book we collect will end up in the hands of a child. For many children, a book can become a close friend, a source of adventure, or even a small spark that ignites a lifetime love of reading. I remember the first time I held a book as a child and the feeling of wonder it brought, how it opened doors to worlds beyond my own. Now, as an author, I can only hope that my books inspire the same curiosity and joy. The Christmas season provides the perfect opportunity to share that experience with little ones who might not otherwise have access to books.

As we gathered our resources and reached out to friends and family, Jeff and I shared our vision for this year's drive. We wanted to make it as memorable and impactful as possible, aiming to collect not just any books, but carefully curated selections that would resonate with children and offer them a meaningful Christmas gift. This year, I felt particularly excited to include several of my own Christmas-themed books in the mix. I hoped the stories would remind children of the magic of the season and the beauty of giving and kindness, values so close to my heart and central to the spirit of Christmas.

Throughout the day, we collected an incredible variety of books, from storybooks with enchanting illustrations to classics that never lose their charm. We were overjoyed to see the generosity pouring in from our community, with so many people contributing new or gently used books. As the stacks grew higher, I couldn't help but marvel at how powerful a book can be. Each one holds potential: to lift spirits, to teach important lessons, and to make children feel seen and valued. Watching our little book mountain grow, I felt an overwhelming sense of gratitude that this simple idea of a book drive had flourished into such a community-supported endeavor.

Once we had all the books, we gathered some wrapping paper, ribbons, and stickers to add a festive touch to each gift. For Jeff and me, this was one of our favorite parts—transforming each book into a Christmas present that a child could unwrap with excitement and anticipation. As we wrapped, we talked about the impact these books might have, imagining each child's face lighting up as they opened their gift. This, to us, was Christmas in action: spreading joy and hope one book at a time, letting each child know that they were thought of and cared for.

Reflecting on the day, I realized just how precious these book drives had become to me. They are more than a holiday event; they are a way to spread love, joy, and encouragement, to connect with children in a meaningful way, and to share the light of Christ. In every story shared, in every wrapped book, there is a message of hope and a reminder of the real reason for the season. Through this book drive, I am blessed to be a vessel for Him, bringing the love of Christ to the little ones in ways that are simple yet profound.

As Jeff and I prepared to distribute the books, I felt a deep sense of fulfillment. This book drive had become a Christmas tradition for us, one that reminded me of the purpose behind each word I write, each book I create. It is my prayer that each child who receives a book will find not just entertainment, but encouragement, inspiration, and the joy of knowing that they are loved. In the end, these simple acts of giving and sharing are the heart of the Christmas spirit, a reflection of God's love for us and a reminder that, in giving, we too are blessed beyond measure.

There's something incredibly special about giving books as gifts, especially during the holidays. Books are timeless, each one holding within it a unique world, a lifetime of knowledge, or a spark of inspiration that can be cherished again and again. I truly believe that giving a book is like giving a piece of one's heart, a gift that never expires and can be revisited anytime. The beauty of a book lies in its power to connect people across generations and backgrounds, and it brings me so much joy to know that, in giving books, I am sharing something that has the potential to impact others in ways that go far beyond the pages.

This season, as Jeff and I prepared our holiday book drive, I couldn't help but reflect on my own love for literacy and the role that books have played in my life. I've been incredibly blessed to have written over 100 books, all by the grace of God, and each time I pen a new story or message, I feel like I'm adding to a collection that God intended to reach different people in unique ways. For me, books are more than just stories or information. They are bridges to understanding, vessels of compassion, and tools for transformation. They bring people together, creating connections between those who read them and those who wrote them. Knowing that one of my books might become a beloved memory for a child, or a comfort to an adult, brings a sense of purpose to my work that I cherish deeply.

Every December, Jeff and I pour our hearts into our book drive, and it's become one of our most beloved traditions. This project feels like an extension of my calling as an author, allowing me to share the joy of reading with children and families who may not have easy access to books. There's something profound about watching people come together to donate books, each one bringing with it the potential to inspire, uplift, and educate. It warms my heart to think that a child's Christmas could be brightened by a single story, one that might stay with them for years to come.

When I think about the timeless nature of books, I am reminded of the ways they accompany us throughout our lives. A beloved children's book might become a comfort during uncertain times, a thought-provoking novel might inspire a young adult to pursue their dreams, and a faith-based book might offer encouragement when someone needs it most. This is what makes books so special and such a meaningful gift to share. They aren't just bound paper; they're experiences, wisdom, and comfort that we can return to time and time again.

There is also something wonderful about gifting a book that carries the spirit of Christmas within its pages. This season, Jeff and I included several Christmas-themed books in our drive, hoping to share the joy, love, and hope that are at the heart of the holiday. Through stories that celebrate the miracle of Christ's birth, the power of generosity, and the warmth of family, we are able to spread messages that resonate with the true meaning of Christmas. Books like these don't just entertain; they instill values, encourage kindness, and remind readers of the love that Christ has for each of us.

Books have always been a treasure in my life, and I know that they have the power to bless the lives of others as well. The act of giving a book, particularly during the holiday season, feels like planting a seed that may grow and flourish in someone's life in unexpected ways. For a child, receiving a book as a gift could be the start of a lifelong love for reading or a journey of discovery and imagination. For an adult, a book could offer insight, solace, or even a shift in perspective that brings peace and clarity.

In a world that often moves too fast, books encourage us to slow down, to reflect, and to connect with ideas, stories, and perspectives that we may not encounter in our daily lives. They offer us a quiet space in which to think, dream, and feel, and this is a gift that is truly priceless. Giving books during the holidays is a way of sharing these blessings with others, a way of saying, "Here's a little piece of joy, a story to keep you company, a lesson to carry with you."

I am grateful to God for allowing me to be a vessel through which stories can flow. Writing books for children and adults alike has been one of the greatest privileges of my life. It feels like a gift to be able to contribute to the world in a way that fosters literacy, inspires creativity, and celebrates the power of words. Each book drive Jeff and I organize is a testament to this love for literacy, a celebration of the countless ways that books can touch lives, and a reminder that the gift of reading is one that can truly change the world.

As I consider the impact of our book drive and the love for literacy that it embodies, I am reminded that books are not only gifts to be given but also legacies to be shared.

Read To The Elderly

Reading aloud to the elderly on this ninth day of December fills me with such a sense of purpose and joy, especially during this special season of Christmas. Yes, I have to admit—I absolutely love books, and I deeply cherish the gift of literacy. There's something magical about reading aloud, sharing words that uplift and inspire, and watching faces light up with memories or the pure enjoyment of a story. Giving the gift of time and a good story feels like the perfect way to celebrate the spirit of Christmas and bring a little extra warmth to those who might be feeling the sting of loneliness this time of year.

When I think about reading to the elderly, my heart swells with excitement, knowing that this simple act can be so meaningful. So often, we forget that stories have the power to heal and connect us in unexpected ways. Many elderly individuals might not have the ability to read as they once did, or they may no longer be able to hold a book comfortably, due to arthritis or diminished eyesight. For some, books used to be close companions, filling countless hours with joy and adventure. So, to share a story with them now is a way of reigniting that joy, of bridging the gap between who they were and who they are, and simply bringing a bit of light into their day.

Jeff and I talked about this idea, and we both agreed that reading aloud during this time of year could be such a blessing. It's a beautiful way to honor the elderly, to make them feel seen and valued. We wanted to choose stories that were rich with Christmas cheer, filled with messages of hope and love that reflect the meaning of the season. Whether it's a Christmas classic, a cozy winter tale, or a devotional that touches on the birth of Christ, each selection can offer something comforting, something meaningful that connects them to the Christmas spirit. Reading aloud is a gift both to the listener and to the reader. As I read, I find myself immersed in the words, fully present in the moment, and it's a unique kind of joy to see the story come alive in the eyes of those listening. It's rewarding to watch their expressions change, to hear them laugh at a humorous line, or to see their eyes fill with emotion during a touching scene. These moments remind me that books truly are timeless, capable of touching hearts regardless of age. And perhaps the best part is that by reading aloud, we're sharing more than just a story; we're sharing companionship, empathy, and a connection that transcends generations.

The power of reading lies in its ability to engage our imaginations, to invite us into worlds beyond our own, and to remind us that we are not alone. This is especially important during the Christmas season when loneliness can be particularly painful. For some elderly individuals, the holidays may bring a sense of loss or longing for loved ones who are no longer with them. But a good story, read with warmth and kindness, can offer comfort and remind them of the joy of Christmases past and the promise of peace and love in the present.

As I sat with a group of elderly individuals, each one wrapped in their cozy holiday blankets and sipping warm tea, I began reading a beloved Christmas story. I could see the nostalgia wash over them, each line bringing forth memories of their own holiday traditions, perhaps scenes of their own children opening gifts under a twinkling tree, or family gatherings filled with laughter. Some even closed their eyes, as though they were letting the words carry them back to those special times. I felt blessed to be the one sharing these moments with them, humbled by the chance to give them this small gift of remembrance and warmth.

Afterward, several of them shared stories of their own holiday memories, from baking gingerbread with their mothers to singing carols in the church choir. It became more than just a reading; it became an exchange of experiences, a celebration of Christmas memories that each of us carried. And in that room, filled with laughter, storytelling, and shared memories, I felt the true spirit of Christmas alive and well.

Reading aloud to the elderly has a way of turning simple words into a balm for the soul. It is an act of kindness, a reminder that they are not forgotten, and a moment to celebrate life's simple joys together. As I continue this tradition, I hope to bring more stories, more laughter, and more warmth to each person I read to. The Christmas season is about giving, but it is also about receiving the incredible joy that comes when we give of ourselves. For me, this day of reading was a gift as much for myself as it was for them, a reminder that in giving, we are also blessed.

There's a scripture that has always resonated with me, especially during the Christmas season: "Truly I tell you,

whatever you did for one of the least of these brothers and sisters of mine, you did for me" (Matthew 25:40, NIV). Every time I read these words, I am reminded of the deep love and compassion Jesus has for everyone, particularly those who may be forgotten or left behind. This verse touches my heart because it shows that when we serve others—whether it's comforting a friend, feeding the hungry, or sitting with the elderly to read to them—we're not just helping people in need; we're honoring Christ Himself. This truth adds so much meaning to the act of reading aloud to the elderly, especially during this beautiful season of Christmas.

When I sit down to read to someone who may be feeling lonely or isolated, I think about this scripture and how God is present in each of these small acts of love. It's easy to overlook these gestures, thinking that they're insignificant or small, but in God's eyes, they are precious. Reading aloud may seem like a simple act, but to someone who is longing for connection, who perhaps feels a bit lonely during the holidays, it can be a profound gift. Through each word I read, I feel that I am, in a small way, sharing the love of Christ with someone who needs it. I am reminded that every page turned, every story shared, is an offering to God, a way of spreading His light in a world that can sometimes feel cold or disconnected.

This Christmas season, as Jeff and I visit with elderly friends and neighbors, I hold Matthew 25:40 close to my heart. I know that these moments of giving, no matter how simple they may seem, are sacred. It's humbling to think that in serving the elderly, we're not just bringing them joy or company; we're connecting with Christ in a tangible way. Through these moments, I'm reminded that Jesus cares deeply about each of us, especially those who might be feeling forgotten. He sees every act of love, and He is honored by our willingness to reach out and make someone's day a little brighter.

This scripture brings such peace and purpose to each visit. As I read a story aloud, I imagine that Jesus is there in the room with us, smiling, enjoying the story right along with everyone else. There's a warmth in knowing that He is present in each gesture of kindness, that He celebrates our desire to bring joy to those who may feel alone. Sometimes, I think about the many ways Jesus Himself showed love and compassion for others, particularly those who were marginalized or overlooked. His love was always active, always reaching out to the "least of these" with a heart full of empathy and grace. To follow His example, even in small ways, feels like a blessing beyond words.

What I find so beautiful about this scripture is that it reveals God's deep appreciation for acts of service that we might consider small. Reading to the elderly may not seem like a grand gesture, but in God's eyes, it is an act of love and respect, a way of showing that each person is valuable and cherished. I think about how God sees the loneliness that some of the elderly may feel, especially during the holidays when memories of lost loved ones and distant family may weigh heavily on their hearts. Through these visits, I feel that we are serving not just with our voices, but with the love and compassion that God has placed in our hearts.

I can't help but feel that in these moments, when we sit together to share a story, it's as though we are creating a space where God's love is tangible, where His presence can be felt in the laughter and smiles that arise. Each time I read a Christmas story, or share a devotion that reminds us of the joy and hope of Christ's birth, I feel a sense of connection not only to the person in front of me but to God Himself. There's something special about knowing that by spending time with those who may feel overlooked, we are honoring Jesus, bringing His love and light into a world that needs it.

As I continue this tradition, I am constantly reminded of the ways in which God honors even the smallest gestures of love. He sees each visit, each story shared, as a reflection of His own compassion. Knowing this fills my heart with gratitude and motivates me to keep giving, to keep reaching out in love, because I know that in doing so, I am honoring the One who has loved me so deeply. This verse from Matthew serves as a beautiful reminder that every act of kindness, every moment spent caring for others, is a form of worship, a way of giving thanks for the love and grace that Christ has given us.

Each Christmas season, as we read stories and share moments of joy with those who need it most, I am reminded of how meaningful it is to serve others, to be a light in someone's life. It's a gift to be able to share this time, to bring a sense of peace and joy into the lives of those who may be feeling isolated. I am grateful for the opportunity to serve, knowing that through each word read and each story shared, we are honoring Christ and spreading His love in a way that brings us all closer together.

Christmas Caroling

Christmas caroling is truly one of those cherished holiday traditions that brings people together in a special way. There's something magical about gathering with friends, family, or even church members, bundling up in coats and scarves, and heading out into the cold winter night with song sheets in hand. The tradition of caroling goes back generations, filling neighborhoods and communities with the joyful sounds of beloved Christmas hymns and carols. Though it's a tradition that seems to be fading in many places, caroling remains a timeless expression of holiday spirit. I feel such a pull to keep this tradition alive, and I believe that when done thoughtfully and safely, Christmas caroling can be a beautiful gift to the singers and listeners alike.

When I think of caroling, I picture the glow of streetlights reflecting off fresh snow, the cozy warmth of my family and friends by my side, and the sense of excitement and joy that comes with sharing the sounds of Christmas. Caroling, to me, isn't just about singing songs—it's about spreading a message of hope, love, and joy. Every carol tells a story, and every note carries the reminder of the birth of Jesus. It's this purpose, to honor His birth, that makes the carols so meaningful. Singing "Silent Night" or "O Holy Night" under a starry sky feels like a moment of worship, shared with the people around us. And when we sing together, it doesn't matter if every note is perfectly in tune. What matters is the joy and the spirit of Christmas that we're sharing with those who hear us.

It's true that caroling has lost popularity in some areas, especially with our modern busyness and distractions. Sometimes people are hesitant to open their doors to strangers, and others feel uncertain about singing in public. But I truly believe that caroling, when planned well and done safely, can be a source of blessing and connection. It's an opportunity to bring something meaningful into our communities, especially during a time of year when many are searching for joy and connection. When people hear the familiar tunes of "Joy to the World" or "Hark! The Herald Angels Sing," there's often a light in their eyes and a smile that says they've remembered something important—the spirit of the season and the goodness it brings.

One of the wonderful aspects of caroling is that it doesn't require much to make it happen. With just a few willing voices, some song sheets, and warm hearts, we can gather and go out to share the music of Christmas. A small group of friends or family members can be just as powerful as a larger church or community choir. And the beauty is that caroling is so flexible—it can be as simple as stopping by a neighbor's house or as organized as singing at a local park or nursing home. It can be done in a way that feels right for the people involved and for the safety and comfort of everyone.

For me, one of the most touching parts of caroling is seeing the impact it has on those who listen. Some people may be going through difficult times during the holidays—perhaps they're grieving, or lonely, or struggling with life's challenges. A simple carol, sung with love, can touch their hearts and remind them that they're not alone. There's something comforting about hearing "Away in a Manger" or "The First Noel" that transcends words. It brings the warmth of community and the promise of hope. Sometimes, people even join in with us, and that's when I feel the real magic of caroling. In those moments, strangers become friends, and the joy of Christmas is shared in a beautiful, simple way.

Caroling can also be a way to pass down traditions to the next generation. When children and young people join in, they experience the joy of giving through music. They learn that Christmas is not just about receiving gifts but about sharing love and kindness with others. Singing together fosters a sense of belonging and purpose, and it teaches young people that their voices matter. When children see the smiles on the faces of those they sing for, they experience the true meaning of Christmas in a way that will stay with them for years to come. For my family, caroling has been a way to instill those values of giving and connecting, and I hope that as the years go by, they'll carry on the tradition with their own families and friends.

For those who may feel hesitant about caroling, either because it's new to them or because they're shy about singing, I encourage giving it a try. Caroling doesn't require perfect singing; it just requires a willing heart. And caroling

with others makes it even easier—there's a certain courage that comes from singing together. For those who want to organize a caroling event, starting with a small group of friends or a church group can be a wonderful way to begin. It's also helpful to plan in advance, choosing the songs and setting a route to visit specific homes or locations. And, of course, it's essential to be mindful of everyone's safety, especially in today's world. Wearing reflective clothing, staying in well-lit areas, and carpooling to locations are all good ways to ensure a safe and enjoyable experience for everyone involved.

I also think it's important to remember that caroling isn't limited to public streets or door-to-door visits. There are many places where people would appreciate the gift of song—a local hospital, a nursing home, or even a community center. Many people in these places may be spending the holidays away from family, and a visit from carolers can lift their spirits in a way that few things can. Bringing the gift of music to those who may not be able to get out and experience the Christmas season can be an incredibly rewarding experience. For me, those are the moments that make caroling worthwhile.

In a world that can feel increasingly disconnected, caroling reminds us of the power of community and the importance of coming together. It's a way to share our faith, our joy, and our gratitude for the birth of Christ. It's a way to

remind ourselves, and those around us, that Christmas is a time for celebration, reflection, and love. Each time I go caroling, I am reminded of why this tradition has endured for so many years—it's because it brings people together, both singers and listeners, in a spirit of kindness and unity. And in a season dedicated to celebrating the birth of Jesus, what better way to honor Him than by spreading joy and love through song?

Caroling may not be as common as it once was, but I believe that by keeping it alive, we can bring light into the world in a simple yet powerful way. So, as we gather each December to sing songs of joy, hope, and peace, I am grateful for the gift of caroling and the memories it creates. And I hope that more people will join in, carrying forward this beautiful tradition that reminds us all of the true meaning of Christmas.

Serving Hot Cocoa

Serving hot cocoa to neighbors during the Christmas season is one of the simplest yet most wonderful ways to bring people together and share the love of Christ. There's just something about the rich, creamy warmth of hot cocoa on a chilly December evening that brings out the joy of the season. Setting up a hot cocoa stand or hosting a gathering in your home or yard gives neighbors a reason to step out of their usual routines, pause for a few moments, and enjoy the warmth and fellowship that Christmas is all about. It's a chance to create memories, spread joy, and remind everyone of the simple, delicious sweetness that life—and this season—has to offer.

For many of us, hot cocoa is a comforting taste from childhood, bringing back memories of snowy nights and cozy holiday moments. Offering hot cocoa to neighbors, both young and old, feels like inviting them into a space of warmth and nostalgia. It's a way to welcome them with open arms, share a treat, and remind them of the shared connections and values that the season embodies. When people gather around for a cup of cocoa, conversation flows easily, and friendships begin to blossom. In a world where people often pass by one another without much more than a wave, a hot cocoa gathering creates a sense of closeness and community, showing everyone that they are valued and welcome.

This act of sharing cocoa is about more than just serving a warm beverage—it's a way to invite the spirit of Jesus' love into our neighborhoods. Christmas is a time when hearts are open and people are more inclined to give and receive, to gather and connect. And just as Jesus taught us to love our neighbors, sharing cocoa is a simple way to practice this love, fostering a spirit of kindness and hospitality. It's amazing how something as humble as a hot cocoa stand can make people feel seen, appreciated, and cherished. For children, it's a memory that they carry into their own holiday traditions, learning the joy of sharing, warmth, and kindness that can be passed down through the years.

To make the experience even more memorable, consider setting up a few special toppings or add-ins, like marshmallows, peppermint sticks, or whipped cream. Kids (and adults too!) delight in creating their own cocoa masterpieces, and it adds a bit of extra fun to the gathering. You could even create a small "cocoa station" with holiday mugs, napkins, and a selection of toppings to make everyone feel like they're part of something magical. If you have a fireplace or a fire pit, setting up the cocoa nearby can add a cozy element, where everyone can gather, sip their cocoa, and enjoy the warmth of the fire and the camaraderie of the group.

Hosting this kind of event also creates an opportunity to share the true meaning of Christmas with neighbors. If you're comfortable, consider adding a small devotional moment or a short reading from the Christmas story. It doesn't need to be formal; sometimes a few heartfelt words about the hope, love, and joy that Christ brings are all that's needed. Or perhaps you could set up a few verses of Scripture on display near the cocoa stand as a gentle reminder of God's love. These simple gestures open the door for meaningful conversations, allowing people to feel the presence of God in the small, intimate moments of the holiday season.

A neighborhood hot cocoa gathering can become a cherished tradition, something neighbors look forward to year after year. By creating a welcoming, festive environment, you can foster a sense of belonging that extends beyond Christmas. Those small, heartfelt gestures—greeting a neighbor with a warm cup of cocoa, a sincere "Merry Christmas," and a friendly smile—often linger in people's minds long after the season has passed. And for those who may be experiencing loneliness or hardship during the holidays, it could be just the reminder they need that they are loved and cared for.

In a busy world where schedules can keep us apart, a hot cocoa gathering gives everyone a reason to pause, savor the moment, and enjoy the true gifts of Christmas: faith, fellowship, and the sweetness of life. Whether it's a spontaneous event or something planned each year, sharing hot cocoa with neighbors brings a touch of Christ's love to the heart of your community, spreading joy in a way that's both simple and profound. So, as you prepare for

the Christmas season, consider warming up the neighborhood with a cup of cocoa and a whole lot of love.

Christmas Bake Exchange

A Christmas cookie or bake exchange is a delightful way to celebrate the season with friends, family, and neighbors. It's a gathering where everyone bakes their favorite holiday treats and exchanges them with one another, filling the air with laughter, the warmth of togetherness, and the sweet aroma of freshly baked goods. Not only is it a delicious way to enjoy a variety of treats, but it's also a chance to share family recipes, treasured traditions, and the love of Christ with everyone who comes.

Imagine a cozy living room, the table laden with cookies, brownies, spice cakes, and festive holiday bread, each delicately wrapped and ready to be shared. This setting brings together people of all ages and baking abilities, uniting them with a common goal: to spread joy and deliciousness. The beauty of a cookie or bake exchange is that everyone brings something unique—family favorites, regional specialties, or even recipes passed down through generations. And when these treats are shared, the stories behind them often come out, creating a tapestry of memories that binds everyone closer together.

Hosting a bake exchange with a Christ-centered focus brings a deeper meaning to the gathering. For example, before the exchange begins, you could open with a prayer of gratitude, thanking God for His provision, for the friendships that bring everyone together, and for the joy of the season. You might even share a verse that resonates with the act of sharing, like Hebrews 13:16: "Do not neglect to do good and to share what you have, for such sacrifices are pleasing to God." This reminder of giving from the heart and spreading joy aligns beautifully with the purpose of the bake exchange, transforming it into a meaningful celebration of Christ's love.

If you're planning to host the exchange, you might consider adding a few fun touches to make the event feel festive and memorable. Ask each guest to bring their recipe on a card to share, so others can recreate their favorites later. You could also create little tags for each type of treat, with notes about the flavors or origins of the recipe, or even a few words about what Christmas means to the baker. This adds a personal touch and makes the exchange feel like a thoughtful act of sharing rather than simply trading baked goods.

A Christmas bake exchange is also a wonderful opportunity to reach out to those in the community who may be feeling lonely or in need of a little extra joy. Some hosts gather extra treats to deliver to nearby senior centers, families going through difficult times, or local shelters. By extending the exchange beyond the gathering, you spread the sweetness and joy of the season to those who might need it most, reflecting Christ's message of kindness and compassion in a tangible way.

Hosting or participating in a bake exchange reminds us that giving is not only about what we share but how we share it. The thoughtfulness that goes into each batch of cookies, the effort put into wrapping and presenting them, and the joyful spirit of giving—these are the things that make a bake exchange so special. It's about more than just baking; it's about putting our love for others into each treat, making every bite a reminder of God's goodness and the gift of His Son.

Lastly, a bake exchange is a great family-friendly activity that brings joy to kids as much as to adults. Little ones love decorating cookies, packaging treats, and learning about the meaning behind the gathering. They get to see firsthand the beauty of giving and receiving, and they learn that even small acts of kindness, like a simple cookie, can bring happiness to others. This experience teaches the value of generosity and gives families a way to celebrate Christmas together, passing on traditions that children will cherish and perhaps carry forward in their own lives.

In all its warmth, sweetness, and spirit of generosity, a Christmas bake exchange beautifully embodies the message of the season. It encourages us to open our hearts, to celebrate the joy of giving, and to taste and see the goodness of the Lord in each delicious treat. Whether it's a gathering of close friends, family, church members, or even neighbors we're getting to know better, a bake exchange brings people together in a way that's simple yet profound, reminding everyone that we're all part of God's family, bound by His love and the sweetness of fellowship.

Merry Christmas

I sincerely hope this Christmas book brings you abundant joy and inspiration throughout the holiday season. Christmas truly is one of the most delightful times of the year—a season where flavors, laughter, and warmth fill our homes, and the presence of friends and family brings our hearts so much comfort and happiness. There's a delicious quality to this time of year, where everything feels wrapped in sweetness and light. We find ourselves savoring not only the wonderful treats on the table but also the precious moments spent together.

As you turn these pages, my prayer is that you are reminded of the deeper joy of Christmas—the joy that comes from celebrating the birth of Jesus, our Savior. This season, let us remember that the heart of Christmas is Christ, whose love for us knows no bounds and whose grace is freely given. His birth brought light to a world in darkness, and His life continues to shine as a beacon of hope, peace, and love. In the midst of all the festivities, the gatherings, the food, and the fun, may you hold onto the quiet miracle of His love—a gift that never fades and grows only sweeter with each passing year.

Each Christmas tradition, whether it's baking, gathering for a meal, singing carols, or exchanging gifts, carries with it a chance to reflect on the joy we have because of Jesus. I hope this book encourages you to embrace these traditions in ways that fill your heart with gratitude and wonder. May it serve as a reminder that every sweet moment and every shared laugh reflects the blessings God pours into our lives. And as you celebrate, may you also find moments of stillness to feel His presence and reflect on the incredible story of His birth. His love is woven through each day of the season and invites us to experience Christmas as more than a holiday, but as a time of genuine joy and renewal.

Christmas is a gift from God, a season to celebrate all that is good, true, and beautiful in life. My hope is that this book will be a companion to you, offering encouragement, inspiration, and a taste of the love that surrounds us. May it bring you and your loved ones closer together, deepen your appreciation for the gift of Jesus, and make this Christmas truly unforgettable.

One of my favorite traditions each year is finding a church service, concert, Christmas ballet, or program that captures the heart and spirit of the holiday season. There's something so uniquely moving about coming together with others to experience the joy and air of Christmas. Stepping into a beautifully decorated sanctuary or theater, seeing the lights and hearing the first notes of a familiar carol or the soft strains of instruments tuning up—it always stirs my heart and draws me closer to the meaning of the season.

hether it's the uplifting voices of a choir, the elegance of a
let retelling a Christmas story, or the simple warmth of a live
tivity scene, these moments help me to remember why we
ebrate. They're a time to pause and reflect on the incredible
ft of Christ's birth, given to us with such unimaginable love.
; an invitation to remember the One who sacrificed so much
r us, to think of the journey Mary and Joseph took, the star
t led the wise men, and the humble manger that cradled our
Savior.
r me, this tradition is not only about enjoying a beautiful
erformance but also about letting my heart be touched
by the reminder of God's love for us. I look forward to
sharing these experiences with my family and friends,
knowing that each of us can feel connected in spirit.
ttending these events fills the season with such richness
nd joy and brings me back to the heart of Christmas: the
love of Christ. I hope you and your loved ones find
opportunities this December to experience the same
onder, to come together in celebration, and to remember
that Jesus' light shines brightly, even in the midst of
winter's longest nights.

Meet Kim Ruff Moore: Beloved Author,
Storyteller, and Literacy Advocate

- ● Children's Books: *Pebo Pig Prefers Pancakes with Ketchup*, *Pebo Pig Prefers Pizza with Pineapple*, and more
- ● AdultBooks: *I Still Have Joy*, *Never Put All Your Eggs in One Basket Waymaker*, *Girl Mash the Gas*, and more

Kim's books can be found at Walmart, Barnes & Noble, Books-A-Million, Harvard Book Store, and other retailers. She's also a Stellar Award-winning singer-songwriter and part of TheNewConsolers with her husband, Jeffery Moore.

Discover Kim's work at kimruffmoore.com and ruffmooremedia.com

Kim Ruff Moore, author of over 90 books, writes inspiring children's stories and Christian self-help books. Founder of the Please Read Project, Kim donates her books to children and adults who need them most, encouraging literacy for all. Her diverse children's catalog, including the Pebo Pig Prefers series and Suzzie Mocha Series, brings joy to readers everywhere.